Origin
of the
Spiritual
Species

Origin
of the
Spiritual
Species

A Melding of Science, Religion and Metaphysics

L e e   B o n d y

authorHOUSE®

AuthorHouse™
1663 Liberty Drive
Bloomington, IN 47403
www.authorhouse.com
Phone: 1 (800) 839-8640

Published by AuthorHouse 06/15/2015

ISBN: 978-1-5049-1133-7 (sc)
ISBN: 978-1-5049-1132-0 (e)

Library of Congress Control Number: 2015907273

Print information available on the last page.

Any people depicted in stock imagery provided by Thinkstock are models,
and such images are being used for illustrative purposes only.
Certain stock imagery © Thinkstock.

This book is printed on acid-free paper.

I am dedicating this book to my wife Madeline Schultz Bondy who died on May 1, 2014 and as a cradle Catholic followed the Ten Commandments and moral teachings faithfully.

But more importantly, she also followed Christ's 11th Commandment, "Love God with all your being and your neighbor as yourself" and she did indeed, regardless of ethnicity or creed, and she had a wide range of friends & neighbors.

May God rest her soul.

Contents

Preface

Why this treatise? While living in California in the 1950s and with a newly minted degree in Electrical Engineering as well as a high paying job with the Douglas Aircraft Company, I was convinced that the Atheists were correct and that all living beings were a product of evolution.

California at that time was a hot-bed of different religious sects which my wife insisted on examining carefully and I would point out the absurdity of their claims.

Then, one day I was reading the Los Angeles Times newspaper and the headline was the death of a yogi, Paramahansa Yogananda who had died several weeks earlier (March 7, 1952), but there was no evidence of decay in his body. How could this be?

I ended up visiting his Ashram which was nearby to learn more about him. As a result, I purchased his book the "The Autobiography of a Yogi" which was a real awakener and I began to investigate other world religions and the natural world as well.

After a decade of observation and investigation, it became obvious to me that "Intelligent Design" was at play and I spent another two decades examining the interplay of Animal, Vegetable and Mineral relationships.

In addition, I examined Darwin's "Origin of the Species" and it became clear to me that there were too many inconsistencies to have any real validity. As it also became clear that the country's school systems were no longer teaching both "Evolution" and "Intelligent Design" as the two possible origins of Man (Homo-Sapiens) but now opted only for "Evolution" as the correct assumption, I felt it necessary to offer a comprehensive presentation of the real story concerning the origin of Man, not only from the physical standpoint but also as a spiritual entity.

This treatise attempts to point out the Darwin contradictions and the spiritual evolution of mankind. Consequently I have determined that I needed to entitle this document "The Origin of the *Spiritual* Species".

I invite both Atheists & Agnostics to reconsider their positions in light of these findings.

Introduction

All thinking and curious persons have pondered the mysteries of life and living, eg:

1. Where did humans (Homo-Sapiens) come from? When? Why?
2. What is life?
3. Is there life after death?
4. Which religion embodies the whole truth?
5. How will we be judged?

To set the stage for this publication, let me quote from Edouard Schure's book that was published in 1970, entitled "From Sphinx to Christ" (An Occult History). Rudolf Steiner considered Schure to be "One of the best guides for finding the path to the spirit in our day". The Sphinx in Egypt was constructed when Egypt was the center of all spiritual knowledge and has confounded viewers for thousands of years. Quoting from Schure's speculation on what the Sphinx would have to say:

"Behold me", it says. "I am the Nature-Sphinx, Angel, Eagle, Lion and Bull, I have the august visage of a god, and the body of a winged and roaring beast". You the viewer, "have neither my croup, my claws, nor my wings, but your bust resembles mine. Who are you? Whence come you? Whither do you go? Have you risen from the slime of earth, or did you descend from the glowing disk of the sun that now rises gloriously above the mountains of Arabia? -----AS to you, ephemeral being, obscure voyager, fleeting shadow - seek and discover! – or else, despair!"

Finally: (He answers the Sphinx) "It matters not to me by what strange chance I issued from your loins, but, since I have been born, I can escape from your talons, for I call myself Will, Reason, Analysis – and all things bow down before my power. Thus I am your master and you become purposeless. And the triumphant superman beholds himself in the mirror of science. Then he starts back in fear. For he sees himself in the form of a gorilla, with hairy body and prognathous countenance, which sneers at him. The Sphinx responds: "Behold your ancestor! Salute your new god! Foolish man, it says; believing yourself descended from the apes, you would deserve never to rise. Know that your greatest crime is to have murdered God!" The cover art shows the Great Pyramid and the Sphinx which was constructed in 10,000 BC.

Although many intellectuals scoff at the legitimacy of a spiritual universe, science is moving ever closer to the world as defined by both religion and metaphysics. The debate continues between Darwin's "Origin of the Species" doctrine and that of Intelligent Design (ID). Hopefully, we can shed some new light on this disagreement.

Peter Hawkins in a recent television series on the origin of the universe concludes with fellow Astro-Physicists that the universe originated from a single energy point - the "Big Bang". Peter also surmised that this energy point originated from some intelligent & universal energy source – although he remains an agnostic or atheist.

Thomas Paine in his publication "Age of Reason" said: "Mystery, miracles and prophecy are the "three frauds' of the Bible". Conversely, Whitehead in "Religion in the Making" said: "You cannot shelter theology from science or science from theology, nor can you shelter either of them from metaphysics, or metaphysics from either of them. There is no shortcut to truth". So if Paine had been a student of science & metaphysics he may have ended the quote with the 'three virtues'. Harvey E. Elliott observed that no religion has a "corner" on virtue. "No religion controls God. Every religious sect is in some way helpful. Helpfulness only is the measure of worth".

Harvey E. Elliott also quoted Tennyson: "It is hard to believe in God; it is harder not to believe in Him". He also went on to say the religionist declares that God is the Creator of all that is. "And who created God," says the materialist? "I don't know," says the religionist. "Nature did it all," says the materialist. "Who created nature?" says the religionist. "I don't know," says the materialist.

Dr. Howard Conn, in a major speech said, "Men and women will always need the great myths to symbolize their personal relationships to a vast unknown that experience has shown to be not empty but resplendent with majestic purposes that run through all civilizations and overleap all distinctions of time. A personal God is the background and sustainer of our groping lives. All of us have kinship with Adam and Eve, with Cain and Abel, with the Tower of Babel and the Cleansing Floods, with Prometheus and Odysseus, with Shiva and Vishnu. These represent creative urges - some beneficent, some destructive - that move deep within us. Religion belongs to the poetry of the human race in those moments when we know that our struggles are more than mundane predicaments, but are indeed the anguish through which something transcendent and eternal shines through each one of us."

The Atheist, since he is sure God does not exist, clings to the Darwinian theory of evolutionary origin for everything – from some primordial soup. The agnostic is not sure and straddles the fence. Here we will explore the alternative – Intelligent Design – as well as the limitations of Darwin's theory.

Yet even the atheist grieves at the grave of a loved one. They should heed the following poem by Mary Elizabeth Frye written in 1932:

> "Do not stand at my grave and weep
> I am not there; I do not sleep.
> I am not there; I did not die"

This publication is intended to provide a bridge between science, theology and metaphysics in exploring the origins of spiritual beings. It contains no mystical revelations to the author but rather excerpts from much more skillful & knowledgeable writers than myself as well as personal observations that science is unable to explain.

The persons who have influenced my search and confirmation of my thoughts on this vast subject are (1)Edgar Cayce (1877-1945) who is undoubtedly the greatest seer of the twentieth century, provides one of the main sources of spiritual insight into the creation and history of the Homo Sapiens, (2) Ruth Montgomery who was a well - regarded journalist and had a psychic guide who helped her publish several books on this subject, including "The World Before", (3) Edward Schure who published the book "From Sphinx to Christ" – an Occult History and (4) Madame Blavatsky whose spiritual insight concurs with the previous authors.

Such is the state of mind which science, without soul, science without God, produces in humanity. Thence arises the two doctrines of agnosticism and materialism which rule the mentality of the present day. Agnosticism says: "Ignoramus, we shall never know the cause of things; let us cease to trouble about it". Materialism says: "There is nothing beyond matter and instinct; let us make the best of it" Others again return to the dogmas of the Church, and, without understanding them, seek consolation in her rites; whose evocative magic is being lost, together with their sublime significance. These rites can still allay uneasiness, but they cannot bestow truth. Edgar Cayce said, "Every Church has value but the real church is in your heart, nonetheless attending your Church regularly provides discipline & fellowship"

Chapter I

Genesis Revisited

Judeo-Christian Genealogy of Man

Edgar Cayce, the most prominent American mystic & prophet (1877-1945), who had the uncanny ability while in trance to access the "Akashic Record" (Book of Life), has shed some new light on the origin of the earth and its species. This provides some new insight into the Bibles creation story or Genesis. Cayce noted that the substance of Genesis was drawn from extant, ancient manuscripts, and from information Moses obtained while in deep states of meditation. In addition, *Joshua*, an aide to Moses, possessed psychic powers and assisted in the interpretation of both the mystic and historical materials.

Cayce does not disagree with the Bible per se, but offers a more realistic look at the seven days of creation. This has always been a controversial concept since it flies in the face of scientific logic and investigation. He has provided clarification of a fuzzy subject.

In addition to discomfort with the creation story, most readers are puzzled by the origin and history of the five races of man which seems to be lacking in our Old Testament. Since this Bible seems to concentrate only on the Semitic tribes,, we are left to wonder about God's relationship with the other tribes of man during this same period.

This section is an attempt to fill in some of these gaps by using information from various sources e.g.; that gleaned from science, the Edgar Cayce readings, other writers and other mystics.

1

Again, this is not an attempt to discredit biblical passages in any way but only offers complementary information that may be useful in understanding the evolution of the human race (both physical & spiritual) and the planet on which we live.

CREATION

The following version of the creation story was derived primarily from the Edgar Cayce readings and differs slightly from popular bible renditions. Keep in mind that many humans were involved in compiling the biblical "Genesis" based upon many "word of mouth" recollections of the teachings of Moses.

"God, the First Cause, moved, and the Spirit came into activity. In the movement, it brought Light. Then chaos".

The projection of Light was synonymous with the Universal Consciousness in association with its companion, Spirit. Thus a spiritual universe (Heaven) was formed requiring neither time nor space nor individual expression. God's first born Son - the Mind, the Word and the Light - was created before the material world. This Master Soul became known as the *"Christ"*.

Before the material world, seven Archangels were created by the will of the Son - the first of these was Lucifer, the Prince of Light, and the second was Michael, who became chief captain of the hosts and Lord of the Way. Also created by the will of the Son were multitudes (trillions) of Mind-born sons in His image which meant they were celestial thought-forms or divine cells in the Body of God (you and me). No others have been created since.

Unfortunately, Lucifer challenged God as the supreme ruler of the spiritual universe and he said, "I will set my throne over against His throne, and I will be as He is". Subsequently, Lucifer was cast out of Heaven with his subordinate angels, into "chaos" or the abyss. In the Gospel of Luke, Jesus recalls Lucifer's rejection - "I beheld Satan as lightning fall from heaven". He became known thereafter as the Prince of Darkness, the Devil, Satan or that Old Serpent.

Edgar Cayce described chaos as being a separate universe created by God as the infinite moved upon the finite in that place outside of itself. In the Hindu (East Indian) literature God is identified as Brahma and they state that their God initiates the "cycle of necessity' by dropping the Cosmic Egg into chaos, from which the visible universe is hatched into being.

Thus ended the "first day of creation" and in Brahmic terms a God-measured day is about a billion years. Again there is dispute over original translations of days, eons or periods of time.

On the "second day of creation" God created our Universe including the Earth and He separated the sky from the waters of the earth. This is an aftermath of the scientific "Big Bang" theory.

On the "third day of creation" God created our own sun & moon and the other stars became visible. In other words, out of this vast scattering clouds of mindless matter –hydrogen gas and dust – emerge the earliest forms of life as wheeling galaxies take shape in flight. Now stars and moons and planets sow themselves in the rapidly expanding, virgin fields of time and space, where they are given initial nourishment by crashing asteroids and the lashing tail of interstellar comets. Then, night and day became known.

On the "fourth day of creation" God separated the earth water from the earth land and created all species of vegetation.

On the "fifth day of creation" God created all species of sea creatures and all species of winged creatures.

On the "sixth day of creation" God created all species of animals.

W.H. Church in his book "Story of the Soul" noted, "Evolution, it has been rightly said, does not create anything, it only reveals it. Its origins lie outside of matter, in the Mind of the Creator. The evolution of all ideas took place in God-consciousness first, before materializing. Evolution in the physical universe got its visible start when Spirit first pushed into matter, in coordination with the creative, energizing forces of Mind (God), becoming what we see in this three-dimensional world of ours as the three kingdoms of the earth, the mineral, the vegetable, and the animal, in their various stages of expression. Each of these three lower kingdoms, in turn, preceded man (the lord of creation) in their arrival here. And each was, and is, imbued with the spirit-force - but not the soul. The soul-force was reserved for man alone".

Within each of the three lower kingdoms, we find what Cayce termed "a 'group mind,' or collective intelligence. It is only man, who has been gifted by the Maker with the three-tiered intelligence embodied in the subconscious, conscious, and super-conscious forces."

On the "seventh day of creation" God rested and blessed the earth and all its inhabitants. To once again quote W.H. Church, "It is rather late in the Brahmic seventh day - though not yet time for Adam's arrival and earth has long been settled in its orbit. Already it is evolving the material manifestations of life, up through the Mesozoic era, and on into the Tertiary period of our own Cenozoic era - geological terms that may mean little enough to the layman, but which imply a time only some millions of years distant from the present, as compared with earth's multi-billion-year-old history."

God had created this world for the pleasure of his Mind-born sons in their spiritual state of existence but He also gave them free will and eventually some decided to join the material state of this world by entering into various animal bodies (about 10 million years ago). Ruth Montgomery, in "The World Before", quoted her spirit guides, "Some of these curious souls experienced the thrill of eating berries, fruits and nuts for a time, and then withdrew to spirit form, leaving the animals unmolested. Others so greatly enjoyed the experience of procreating, eating and sleeping that they became entrapped, and were unable to leave these gross physical bodies."

Thus the "fall from spirituality" (original sin) and the resulting mixtures of animals & man in the Earth began. Again, quoting Ruth Montgomery's guides, "Their misshapen offspring had partly human bodies with such appendages as cloven hooves, tails, horns, fins or feathers." They were known in Genesis as the "sons and daughters of men". This was in contradiction to God's wishes but since he had given his Mind-born sons free will, the fall into materiality became a fact. Cayce noted, "The loss of the First Consciousness, or Divine Awareness, was the result of rebellion. The spirit of selfishness is symbolized in Lucifer, Satan, the Devil, and the Serpent. They all are one - spiritual rebellion."

Eventually, God's first-born son (the Mind, the Word and the Light), who was then known as Amelius (in spirit form only), agreed to enter the Earth plane (or materiality) and begin a race of men that suited God's wishes. Quoting Ruth Montgomery's guides once again, "It was thus that the force we call God decided to form, first in thought and then in matter, a superior creature with hands and feet and sturdy upright bones, and with a mind larger in proportion to the body who could distinguish good from evil. After human souls were separated into male and female so they could reproduce their own kind (Sons of God), God imposed Divine laws making it impossible for human beings to produce offspring as a result of cohabitation with any other species." This probably occurred by redesign of the prior genetic code.

Accordingly, the "Adamic" race was established and Robert Krajenke, author of "Edgar Cayce's Story of the Old Testament", noted, "Since the <u>fall</u>, when spiritual energy became sexual energy, the descendants of Adam were dedicated to the purification and restoration of man's creative potential". The battle between physical desires and spiritual desires began.

In fact, five races of man (Homo- Sapiens) were established simultaneously (mystics indicated that 144,000 souls entered into each race group) in various parts of the world about 5 million years ago as follows:

1. The White Race developed in the Caucasus area along the Black Sea and Carpathian Mountains of Central Europe (Iran).
2. The Yellow Race developed in what is known today as the Gobi Desert of East Asia (China)
3. The Black Race developed in the Sudan & upper West Africa.
4. The Brown Race developed in the Andes & Lemuria (the continent that once existed in the area of the Pacific Ocean).
5. The Red Race developed in the legendary Atlantis (a land mass that once existed along the East coast of North America & Southeastern America extending East to the African West coast.

THE MELTING POT BEGINS

Adam and Eve were symbols in all of the five races and all were members of the "perfect" race of peoples. According to Ruth Montgomery's guides,

"The Garden of Eden was a figurative place located on no particular landmass, as the entire earth in the Adam-Eve days was green and verdant, without ugliness or barrenness. The snake was merely a symbol for the Kundalini (the creative power which lies coiled like a serpent at the base of the spine, until awakened) and the forbidden fruit was the opening of the seven chakras (the psychic centers, or ductless glands) too suddenly, with stress on the gonads (the earthly center) rather than the pineal (the Christ center) and the pituitary (the master gland, or God force) – otherwise spiritual energy became sexual energy. For more information on this subject I recommend that you read the book "The Astral Body" by A.E. Powell & published by The Theosophical Publishing House in Wheaton, Illinois.

They lived, multiplied and adapted to the environments in which they were created but eventually migrated into territories of other races in varying degrees, resulting in a wide range of mixtures and cultures.

According to Ruth Montgomery, "All psychic sources agree that the lost continent of Mu, or Lemuria, was the cradle of civilization. The guides describe it as a mighty landmass extending from the northern reaches of California to the tip of Peru, and encompassing a vast Pacific area of which Hawaii, Tahiti, Polynesia and Easter Island are remnants. Now on Mu there lived a holy one who shed light on the path for others. The archetype of the human race, his name was Amelius, and he was so light (spirit body only) that he could appear almost simultaneously in any part of the earth. This was the first appearance on earth of the "Christ Spirit." Lemuria was the birthplace of the Brown race and some 40,000 years ago most of this landmass sank into the Pacific Ocean, but not before many had migrated to Asia and South America.

The other great landmass of antiquity was Atlantis, the birthplace of the Red race, which stretched from the East-rim of the Americas, including coastal parts of Georgia, the Carolinas, Virginia, the West Indies and Brazil, across what is now ocean to the west coast of Africa. This land was the subject of Plato's account of a lost continent as depicted in the Greek works of "Critias" and "Timaeus". As did Lemuria, Atlantis sank into the Atlantic Ocean about 11,000 years ago. Quoting W.H. Church concerning the remains of Atlantis, "This points us in the direction of the Azores. Are they perhaps a mountainous Atlantean remnant, once submerged and now risen again, along with Madeira and the Canary Islands, further to the south and east?"

Thus, through the Christ spirit, the Holy Spirit in Adam - in man as a race (Homo-Sapiens) - a way was prepared for the conquest of the world; the conquest of spirit over matter, good over evil. Hence, Adam as an individual as well as a group (all men), started humanity on the long journey back to the Creator.

Following is Edgar Cayce's timetable for events associated with the early development of the Homo Sapiens:

1,000,000-800,000 B.C. = Early Lemurian development
    500,000 B.C. = Lemuria partially inundated by water, people scatter
400,000-300,000 B.C. = Lemuria inhabited & civilization advanced
    250,000 B.C. = Second Lemurian catastrophy (Fire?)
    200,000 B.C. = Early Atlantean culture emerged
    80,000 B.C. = Final Lemurian submergence
    28,000 B.C. = 2nd Atlantean submergence (Great Flood)
    10,700 B.C. = Final sinking of Atlantis
    10,390 B.C. = Completion of the Great Pyramid (Egypt)

All races developed religions that were based upon the original one God concept but with different methods of worship and different deities. Over time, man's ego diluted the one God concept and various forms of idol worship were interspersed with the original form of worship. In other words, material desires began to supersede spiritual desires.

Our Judeo Christian tradition is based upon the history of a specific group of people - the Jewish people traced to the man, Abraham, and his descendants to the time of *Jesus Christ* (henceforth the Master Soul, the Christ Spirit shall be italicized).

Adam and Eve of the Caucasus had three children - Cain, Abel and Seth. Cain slew Abel and was banished. The offspring of Cain were known as the sons of Belial. The Judeo-Christian "Genesis" we know traced the descendants of Seth which included *Enoch,* Methuselah, Noah and Abraham (Abram).

In Edgar Cayce's Story of the Old Testament by Robert W. Krajenke, it was noted; "Just as the descendants of Cain obtained their vocations through their dependency upon the earth, the children of Seth were to practice man's other vocation, religion. They were to be guided and sustained by that which came from within, and to live in the manner as the spirit directed."

Enoch lived some 11,000 years B.C. and may have been known as Hermes, who was considered the architect of the Great Pyramid of Cheops. According to Cayce, *Enoch* was a manifestation of the Christ Spirit and acted as a prophet who also warned of the impending deluge (flood) if the people of the world did not conform to God's ways.

The eighth descendent of Adam was Methuselah who was one of the last to live to an age of 1,000 years,

Noah was the next noteworthy descendent of Adam by Seth, and who was considered by God to be the only perfect man in his day & generation. Noah along with seven other souls were spared by God during the Great-Flood (Noah's Ark). This occurred some 30,000 years ago when Atlantis was submerged during a great cataclysm.

As Noah's descendants multiplied in the earth and formed large groups, they embraced self-gratification, power and idol worship as well as material worship. A Cayce reading referred to this development, "Thus when man began to defy God in the earth and the confusion arose which is represented in the Tower of Babel - these are the representation of what was then the basis, the beginnings of nations. Nations were set up then in various portions of the land, and each group, one stronger than another, set about to seek their gratifications".

Also, as a consequence, God thereafter cut man's normal life span to 120 years from the original 1,000 years. It subsequently became necessary for a singular nation to be raised to serve God and Abram (Abraham) was chosen as the father of this people, God's people.

Although a common language existed for all the races of people in the beginning, God also established a multitude of varying languages among the evolving nations to reduce the exploitation of weaker populations (Tower of Babel).

Chapter II

Darwinism Revisited

Charles Darwin in his 1859 publication "On the Origin of Species" caused public controversy that continues today. He was a 22-year old amateur naturalist who spent five years on a British research ship the HMS Beagle and always went ashore to study various plant & animal species whenever the ship anchored at a multitude of destinations. He was particularly noted for his records taken on the islands of the Galapagos showing similar animal species inhabiting South America but with small differences between each island. He concluded that differences were related to adaptations in accordance with the survival of the fittest. He was convinced that all animal life originated from single-celled life forms dating back millions of years thus resulting in the Homo Sapiens (Man) of today.

Quoting directly from his above publication in his Introduction he devotes the first five chapters to natural selection and how any selected variety will propagate to new and modified forms and the complex and little known laws of variation. In the five succeeding chapters he will discuss the most apparent difficulties of his theories – which I will quote directly from his publication as follows:

1. "Still less do we know of the mutual relations of the innumerable inhabitants of the world during the many past geological epochs in its history. Although much remains obscure, and will long remain obscure, I can entertain no doubt, after the most deliberate study and dispassionate judgment of which I am capable, that the view which most naturalists until recently entertained, and which I

formerly entertained, and which I formerly entertained – namely that each species has been independently created – is erroneous. (*Completely contrary to the Intelligent Design concept*).

2. We have also what are called monstrosities; but they graduate into varieties. By a monstrosity I presume is meant some considerable deviation of structure, generally injurious, or not useful to the species. ------- It may be doubted whether sudden and considerable deviations of structure, such as we occasionally see in our domestic productions, more especially with plants, are ever permanently propagated in a state of nature. Almost every part of every organic being is so beautifully related to complex conditions of life that it seems as improbable that any part should have suddenly produced perfect, as that a complex machine should have been invented by man in a perfect state. (*Would seem to apply to the Intelligent Design concept*).

3. There is no exception to the rule that every organic being naturally increases at so high a rate, that, if not destroyed, the earth would soon be covered by the progeny of a single pair. Even slow-breeding man has doubled in twenty five years, and at this rate, in less than a thousand years, there would literally not be standing room for his progeny. (*This has been an issue for hundreds of years, that the population of Homo Sapiens would soon increase beyond the ability to sustain them*). Long before the reader has arrived at this part of my work, a crowd of difficulties will have occurred to him. Some of them are so serious that to this day I can hardly reflect on them without being in some degree staggered. These difficulties and objections may be classed under the following heads; first, why, if species have descended from other species by fine graduations, do we not everywhere see innumerable transitional forms? Secondly, is it possible that an animal having, for instance, the structure and habits of a bat, could have been formed by the modification of some other animal with widely different habits and structure? Can we believe that natural selection could produce, on one hand, an organ of trifling importance, such as the tail of a giraffe, which serves as a fly-flapper, and, on the other hand, an organ so wonderful as the eye? (*More confirmation of Intelligent Design*).

4. But, as by this theory innumerable transitional forms must have existed, why do we not find them imbedded in countless numbers

in the crust of the earth? I will here only state that I believe the answer mainly lies in the record being incomparably less perfect than is generally supposed. The crust of the earth is a vast museum; but the natural collections have been imperfectly made, and only at long intervals of time. But I will pass over this way of escaping from the difficulty; for I believe that many perfectly defined species have been formed on strictly continuous areas. (*It should be noted that recent discoveries have found complete museum bones of dinosaurs and their ages predated Darwin's assumption of early evolutionary organisms as well as early sea creatures*).

5. With regard to the origin of the animal eye, in particular to the perfection of the Eagles eye, although another scientist (*Mr. Wallace*) insist it is highly unlikely that it could occur by natural selection (*evolution*) since such a marvelous organism would require simultaneous changes. To arrive, however, at a just conclusion regarding the formation of the eye, with all its marvelous capabilities, yet with not absolutely perfect characters it is indispensable that reason should conquer the imagination, but I have felt the difficulty far too keenly to be surprised at others hesitating to extend the principle of natural selection to so startling a length. (*Another attempt to explain away the evidence of Intelligent Design*).

6. No complex instinct can possibly be produced through natural selection, except by slow and gradual accumulation of numerous slight, yet profitable variations. He must be a dull man who can examine the exquisite structure of the Bee's comb, so beautifully adapted to its end, without enthusiastic admiration. We hear from mathematicians that bees have practically solved a recondite problem, and have made their cells of the proper shape to hold the greatest amount of honey, with the least consumption of precious wax in their construction. Then Darwin goes on to say, "All this beautiful work can be shown, I think, to follow from a few simple instincts". (*See chapter III of this book to learn how instincts are inherited at birth for all species*).

The intellectual elite with science backgrounds insist that Intelligent Design (ID) is nonsense and that science knows or will know that Darwinism is the whole truth and nothing but the truth. A principle proponent of this theory is Richard Dawkins of Oxford University who insists that a close reading of current evidence should lead one to become an atheist. Another proponent of ID is Francis Collins, who is the Director of the National Human Genome Research Institute, who believes that God cannot be completely contained within nature and therefore God's existence is outside of science's ability to weigh in. As an example, Collins said both of them agree that there are six or more universal constants that if they had varied at all, life would have been impossible as we know it – if one of these, the gravitational constant, were off by one part in a hundred million the expansion of the universe after the big bang would not have allowed such life to occur.

Back to the theory of evolution, if the earth is about 4.5 Billion years old and was only inhabitable by any life form within the last billion years, a lot of evolution must have taken place in this period of time to go from a single celled amoeba to the current human form (Homo-Sapiens), although even science admits there is a missing link from pre-historic ape men to today's human population. Also, anthropologists have spent centuries unearthing early specimens of Darwin's species and have yet to discover any mutation skeletons as one species would have evolved into the next specie. A particularly interesting new specimen was found in Australia during a later British expedition which they called the "Duck-billed Platypus" but when the specimen was turned over to the Royal Institute of Anthropology it was rejected as a fraud since it did not fit the Darwinian model – yet the Duck-billed Platypus is alive and well to this day in Australia.

Furthermore, since Darwinism speculates that our current human species was just an evolution of the ape family it seems odd that some of the current ape family has not evolved into more intelligent animals. Even young Homo-Sapien children can perform amazing feats, in particular musical genius. Following are some examples of extraordinary skill sets that cannot be explained by brain size alone as evolution would forecast:

1. Albert Einstein – was universally known as the greatest genius of our time and much speculation ensued over his brain size to contain such intelligence. However, after his death and subsequent autopsy scientists were astounded to find his brain was of normal size.
2. Victor Borge – first piano debut at age 8.

3. Franz List – first piano debut at age 9.
4. Wolfgang Amadeus Mozart – first piano & violin debut at age 6.
5. Jascha Heifitz – first violin debut at age 7.
6. Yo-Yo Ma – first cello debut at age 5.
7. Tony DeBlois – born a blind savant in 1974 but could play the piano at age 2 & now in his mid-thirties can play 20 different instruments.
8. Seth F. Henriett – a Hungarian autistic savant born in 1980 could play the flute at age 7 with an IQ of 140 but is considered a genius.

Scientists know that every ocean species requires a food chain to survive and the basic food for the lower forms is Krill which is in abundance. Without Krill there would not be the wide range of species from the Mackerel to Whales. The same is true of land animals and the wide diversity would not be possible without a commensurate food chain.

When we were young we often heard the phrase "Which came first, the chicken or the egg." Mother Nature requires both a female & male of each species to reproduce and therefore the egg could not have been first since it must be fertilized to reproduce. But from what other creature could a pair of chickens have evolved?

The same question should be asked of all creatures from the tiny Mouse to the Elephant and before that the Dinosaurs.

Mother Nature's Trash Service

One of the most amazing stories involves all the creatures created to keep the land-masses clean and orderly. We have a wide variety of insects such as termites, ants & worms that reduce organic materials to compost or the world would be overrun with trash. In addition, there are animals that clean the wild kingdoms of dead bodies including buzzards and hyenas or we would have enormous wild graveyards and of course beetles & worms help with the cleanup.

The same is true of the oceans and water-ways, dead organic materials, if they make it to the bottom, are consumed by a variety of bottom feeders including some of our favorite foods – crabs & lobsters.

Chapter III

God's Intranet

Edgar Cayce, when asked in trance where he obtained the remarkable information about people and events, explained that it came from what he called the Akashic Records which contained the cosmic information about every soul and event since creation. They are vibratory records with unique identification codes for everyone and everything in the universe. They are also known as the memory of nature and the book of life.

All life forms are interconnected through an Akashic Field that acts like a universal intranet, communicating information to and from an intelligent design source (God himself). This means that every thought, word and deed of the human race are recorded for posterity and, in addition, some individuals receive enlightenment from this source which is reflected in their achievements on the earth plane.

The animal world receives information through this field in a collective consciousness vein that directs the group activities of each species including their mating activities, group relationships, migration patterns and protective instincts (it is well known that non-domestic animals receive warnings of impending natural disasters and they automatically seek safe habitats).

Amazing stories abound regarding salmon and some other sea species that return to the exact location of their birth when it is their turn to propagate. It is well known that salmon swim upstream against all odds to reach their original spawning area. Recently a giant female sea turtle was caught in a fishing net off the coast of Mexico and was turned over to a marine biologist who decided to attach a GPS transducer to its back and he with other colleagues tracked its movement via satellite. After several months it proceeded North and then West to a small unpopulated atoll near Japan where local biologists waited for the turtle to come ashore. After some 5,000 miles of travel it laid its eggs in the exact spot where it hatched some years earlier. Surely, the Akashic-Field served as its own GPS.

There are other amazing stories about pets that can find their way home after being removed hundreds of miles from their original home, homing pigeons who can be released many miles from their birth-home and in all kinds of weather can unerringly find their way home and swallows of Capistrano (California) who return from other countries each year on the exact date to nest in this old mission.

How about science and the Akashic- Field? Dr. Ervin Laszlo one of the world's leading scientific investigators in his recent book "Science and the Akashic- Field" explores the relationship of this age-old mystical field to modern scientific research into this information field. He was adequately described by a colleague, Ziv Naveh, PH.D as follows;

"In his admirable 40-year quest for an integral theory of everything, Lazlo has not restricted himself to physics but presented a coherent global hypothesis of connectivity between quantum, cosmos, life and consciousness"

In the forward to his book, he inscribed the following definition of this Akashic Field:

"Akasha is a Sanskrit word meaning ether: all pervasive space. Originally signifying radiation or brilliance. In Indian philosophy Akasha was considered the first and most fundamental of the five elements – the others being vata (air), agni (fire), ap (water) and prithivi (earth). Akasha embraces the properties of all five elements: it is the womb from which everything we perceive with our senses has emerged and into which everything will ultimately re-descend. The Akashic Record (also called the Akashic Chronicle) is the enduring record of all that happens, and has ever happened, in space and time"

Lazlo went on to say, "In their quest to create a theory of everything {TOE), quantum physicists base their mathematics on string and super-string theories that define the physical laws of the universe into a single equation. But they do not take into account that life, mind and culture that are part of the world's reality and a genuine TOE must take them into account as well".

Also, he stated, "We go on to ask questions about the nature of consciousness. Did it originate with Homo Sapiens or is it part of the fundamental fabric of the cosmos?"

In the book Edgar Cayce's "Story of the Soul" compiled by W.H. Church, the author noted that two astonishing new scientific disciplines have recently emerged – one is called the science of chaos, the other the science of experimental metaphysics. These are departures from past scientific dogma of determinism or empirical data only.

Cayce observed that if science could unravel one of the higher mysteries of the universe, the nature of Akasha (the mysterious ether) which is a mental force in its essence and permeates all space.

Further in support of Lazlo,'s research, Niels Bohr, quantum theorist noted that the very act of a human observing the electron in the laboratory can cause it to change its behavior resulting in sudden order out of chaos. The Akashic field again.

One of the most spectacular stories of nature at work relates to the Monarch butterfly, one of the most beautiful of all butterflies, that twice a year migrate from northern Mexico after wintering there for 4 to 5 months (in hibernation). In early summer they move to areas near the Texas-Mexico border seeking new growths of milkweed plants. The females lay one egg on several different plants which hatch into caterpillars within two weeks. Each caterpillar then feeds on the milkweed plant and grows rapidly for about two weeks. They then wrap themselves into a cocoon during the pupa stage emerging within another two weeks into a mature Monarch butterfly. They will feed on available flower nectar to prepare for a long journey ahead and then will join millions of others to migrate to the Northern latitudes (Canada & North-Eastern USA). They inherently know when the milkweed population in these areas will again support the next cycle of rebirth from eggs, to caterpillars to mature butterflies.

Again, an example of individual species guided by the Akashic Field for their specific species.

What is particularly amazing about this story is that on their long migrations (up to 2800 miles) for both winter and summer roosts, these are all newly hatched Monarch butterflies that have never flown these routes before but have some inherent GPS (Akashic Field) that repeats the cycle precisely each year.

Another amazing story involves their arrival in Mexico on their southward journey to warmer roosting sites is the Mexican holiday (Dia de los Muerto) known as the "Day of the Dead" precisely on November 1st & 2nd with the arrival of the bulk of the Monarchs. This is not inconsequential since the locals consider la mariposa Monarca to be the souls of spirits of departed relatives that have returned for an annual visit. Others believe that they are as the doves, or souls of the lost children. The Monarchs consistently arrive on these exact dates.

A similar story is the arrival of swallows in Capistrano (an abandoned Spanish mission in California precisely on the same date & time for their summer nesting.

Chapter IV

You Have Only One Life To Live?

It is well known that many persons have an intuitive feeling that there is some life after death - in spite of scientific and intellectual pronouncements to the contrary. Certainly, most of us have experienced or heard about impressions or communications from beyond the grave. There is a plethora of publications relating to reincarnation, near-death experiences (NDE) and past-life regressions; among them:

1. "Journey of Souls" by Michael Newton, Ph.D.
2. "Echoes from the Battlefield" by Barbara Lane.
3. "Reincarnation – a new horizon in science, religion and society" by Sylvia Cranston & Carey Williams.

In the preface to their book on Reincarnation (above), Cranston & Williams state: "It may interest those who have always dismissed theories of immortality as comforting illusions that reincarnation is often rejected precisely because it is not the 'easy way out'. For instance, consider the fundamentalists and born-again Christians. They prefer an everlasting stay in heaven to the painstaking work of returning to earth to struggle diligently again for their redemption."

Benjamin Franklin at the age of twenty two prepared his own epitaph presumably supporting reincarnation:

The Body of B. Franklin,
Printer,
Like the Cover of an Old Book
Its Contents Torn Out
And
Stripped of its Lettering and Gilding
Lies Here
Food for the Worms,
But the Work shall not be Lost,
For it Will as He Believed
Appear Once More
In a New and more Elegant Edition
Revised and Corrected
by the Author

Kathy Callahan in the January/February 2009 edition of venture Inward reports on one of Cayce's readings that tell us that the soul that incarnated as Ben Franklin was also Arart, the Elder Pharaoh during Cayce's incarnation as Ra Ta. This came from a reading for Mr. Franklin Bradley who was a friend and supporter of Edgar Cayce and his "Work". The reading went on to say that in his incarnation as Benjamin Franklin, "this entity was among those who builded for the good of those to come, ministering in many ways and in many manners to the needs of the nation yet unborn, and many of the words in the verse, in line, are often quoted in schools, in places of learning, in copy. In the name then Franklin. The entity gained through this experience, giving self in service to many".

In most Indian (India) religions including Buddhism, reincarnation is considered fact, not speculation. These practitioners strive to lead ascetic lives and therefore avoid numerous future reincarnations. Permanent residence in heaven (blissful, spiritual existence with God) is their ultimate goal.

Even though Hinduism and Buddhism are the primary examples for the belief in reincarnation, there are some other examples, such as a Mayan stele near the beautiful temples and pyramid of Palenque (South America) who was their ruler in 700AD. On this stele he writes that he is the reincarnation of a prior god known as "G1" (god #1) in a series of gods. In his present incarnation he explains that he is now more human and earthly than in prior incarnation, but fortunately he retains memory of that life.

Charles Eastman, whose American Indian name was Ohiyesa, relates in his book *The Soul of the Indian*, "many of the Indians believed that one may be born more than once; and there were some who claimed to have full knowledge of a former incarnation."

Further, Ernest Thompson Seton referred to the body after death in his book *The Gospel of the Redman*, "They consider it a mere husk, an empty case to be disposed of with view only to the comfort of the survivors. The soul that emerged will go on to the next life, and construct for itself a new and better body."

There is considerable evidence that reincarnation was accepted by many Jewish sects including the Essenes both before and after Christ's entry into this material world. Indeed, Christ alluded to it in many of his pronouncements, eg:

1. Jesus asked his disciples, "Who do men say that the Son of Man is?" They replied, 'Some say John the Baptist, others say Elijah, and others Jeremiah or one of the prophets." But who do you say that I am? (Matthew 16:13-15)
2. The Old Testament concludes with a prophecy, "Behold, I will send you Elijah the prophet before the great and terrible day of the Lord comes." (Malachi 4:5) Jesus identified with this prophecy when the disciples asked, "Then why do the scribes say that first Elijah must come?" He responded, "Elijah does come, and he is to restore all things; but I tell you that Elijah has already come, and they did to him whatever they pleased. So also the Son of Man will suffer at their hands." Jesus was speaking of John the Baptist. *(Matthew 17:10-13)*.

Jesus was saying that Herod's wife Herodias, who hated John, had convinced Herod to cut off his head. It was thought that Herodias was the reincarnation of Jezebel who was the leader of Baal (1Kings 19.2) and John (then Elijah) challenged Jezebel's prophets that he could call on God to bring a fire that would destroy their altar and asked them to do the same first. When the Baal prophets could not succeed, Elijah called down God's fire that destroyed their alter. Elijah subsequently had all of her prophets killed. Jezebel swore she would get even with Elijah for killing her prophets.

3. In chapter 8 of the Gospel of John, Jesus was taunted by the Israelites for setting himself up as greater than Abraham. He replied: "Your father Abraham rejoiced that he was to see my day; he saw it and was glad." The astounded Israelites replied, "You are not yet fifty years old, and have you seen Abraham?" Jesus answered, "Truly, truly, I say to you, before Abraham was, I am."

4. One of the best Western sources for evidence of reincarnation, using scientific approaches, is the University of Virginia's Ian Stevenson who has written nine books on the subject - .
    In his first Book titled "Twenty Cases Suggestive of Reincarnation". and other books he presents 65 of over 2,600 cases of past-life memories from children where reincarnation is accepted and where parents & relatives were cooperative and the results are inescapable.

Past relationships and their present influences are not only true of individuals but also of group relationships. Cayce's readings say that from the beginning, souls have tended to travel in groups. This very fact created forces of attraction that helped maintain and build these group relationships. These deep currents below the surface of consciousness cause us to feel instantly comfortable with one person & uncomfortable with another. Everyone involved in our present life was very likely involved in our past lives.

Soul groups create an affinity among their members through their collective memory of how life has been for them and what they have come to mutually desire from it. Such groups form a distinct collective consciousness and spirit, much like the souls who gave us "the Spirit of 1776" reflecting that soul group's mutual hopes, attitudes, and purposes – resulting in the founding of the United States of America. The same can be said for the generations of WWII. Now we have the generation of "Millennials" which we are now trying to understand.

Cayce reflected on the impact of reincarnation in a person's life, "The great geniuses of today, whether in the arts, science, agriculture, or religion, reflect the manner in which they, as entities - as souls - partook or developed in the beginning. Their 'genius' is the result of a continued involvement with their vocation over many incarnations."

Cranston & Williams related that the Jewish Cabalists - whose teachings prevailed as the dominant thought in the Judaic world for three hundred years - taught that when an individual no longer needs to be reborn for his own progress, he "can out of compassion for the world repeatedly return to help it.....the righteous transmigrate endlessly for the benefit of the universe, not for their own benefit."

Lytle Robinson in his book "Story of the Origin and Destiny of Man" quoted from Dr. Leslie Weatherhead, a respected theologian of City Temple, London, concerning reincarnation, "...the early Christian Church accepted it until the Council of Constantinople in A.D. 553, and then discarded it by a vote of 3 to 2. Even Origen, St. Augustine and St Francis of Assissi accepted it." Robinson continues, "Origen;(A.D. 185-254), one of the leading, early Christian scholars, was among those excommunicated for his views on the immortality of the soul. They were victims of the many Anathemas of the day".

KARMIC BOUYANCY

Karma is a report card for each individual relating to his/her spiritual status. There is both good Karma and bad Karma just as there are passing grades and failing grades. Ruth Montgomery asked her guides when the law of Karma (eye for an eye, tooth for a tooth) went into effect and they responded, "Divine law will not be thwarted and when one violates that law, he must repay, or be cut off from the creative force we term God. This knowledge entered with Amelius and his associates, and so freshly was it engraved on their souls that to violate the law was to fall from grace." The subsequent fall into materiality was addressed by the guides (Ruth Montgomery) as well, "Thus we have reincarnation, the sad story of man returning again and again to physical body, resolved to wash out the evil from his record. Some have advanced sufficiently to complete the wheel of rebirth, and those perfected ones need never return to a physical body."

Karma is related to human desires which are both material (carnal) and spiritual. Persons with essentially spiritual desires have a preponderance of good Karma whilst those with essentially material desires have a preponderance of bad Karma. At the end of each life on earth, an individual's karmic report card will reflect the status of their desire bodies.

Cayce had his own perspective on Karma, "Hence karma, to those disobeying - but making for self that which would be as the tower of Babel, or as the city of Gomorrah, or as the fleshpots of Egypt, or as the caring for those influences in the experience that satisfy or gratify self without thought of the effect upon that which it has in its own relation to the first cause! Hence to many this becomes the stumbling block."

Lytle Robinson in Edgar Cayce's *Story of the Origin and Destiny of Man* comments on the karmic pattern, "Thus people's lives follow a self-made pattern, a karmic pattern of loves, hates, fears, desires; of families, friends, groups and nations. Every soul has its own particular karmic pattern, says Cayce. These are of two types and brought in at birth, which like death is but the transition to another plane of existence. There are those innate mental urges derived from experiences out-of-body in the cosmic realms, and the emotional tendencies resulting from (prior) lives in the earth. The word *interests* most adequately describes the mental inclinations gained from planetary sojourns, while *feeling* best expresses those emotional urges from past physical lives - a kind of sensing or knowing without reason."

Robinson continues, "*Bad* karma is the meeting of debts, the overcoming of deficiencies, the tempering of extremes. It is generated by intemperance, neglect, pride, greed, jealousy, and hate in all its forms. Unless it is met and the motivations behind it overcome, it can be a vicious cycle turning up again and again in the lives of its creator."

Avoiding these influences is simply not possible. Whether we like it or not, the Universal Law of Karma – what Christians understand as "What you sow, you reap"- and our children say "What goes around, comes around" – are constantly before each of us. Our fate is the result of our past use of free will.

Cayce concludes that the pattern of mental enfoldment and good karma is fulfilled through service as, "the willingness to be used to produce that as the Creative Forces would have manifested in a material world.....and the constant desire to be at an atonement with Creative Forces." He continues, "These are the desires that will lead us out of the thrall of the appetites, the senses, or the ego."

Finally, if we become too materialistic, we lose touch with our eternal life, which reaches beyond the temporal one. If we become too spiritually consumed, we lose this incarnation's opportunity to apply in daily life what our soul seeks to resolve and accomplish. If spirit-life were all that our soul desired, then it would not have incarnated in the beginning but would have remained with God as spiritual helpers. The people in this life are key to our soul's growth and the resolution of unfinished business.

In an article for A.R.E. by Herbert Bruce Puryear, PhD, he related karma and a person's unconscious, "Since a portion of ourselves is unconscious, we must begin precisely where we are, with the limitations, weaknesses, habits, inclinations - that which some would call karma - of our present status. From that point of here and now we must begin. The 'Secret of the Golden Flower' says: 'The secret of the magic of life consists in using action in order to attain non-action. We must not wish to leap over everything and penetrate directly. The maxim handed down to us is to take in hand the work on human nature.' What does it mean to use action in order to attain non-action? The Sanskrit word for action is karma. Karma means literally action. Thus we may paraphrase this teaching to say, 'The secret of the magic life consists in using (good) karma in order to attain non-karma'."

To the Buddhist, a good karmic report card will lessen the number of reincarnation cycles one must endure. It is unknown what grade will assure no further reincarnations but I suspect it must be in the honor-grade class. The Bible refers to previous sins (Karma) that can affect someone in the next incarnation:

1. As he (Jesus) passed by, he saw a man blind from his birth. And his disciples asked him, "Rabbi, who sinned, this man, or his parents, that he was born blind?" Jesus answered, "It was not that this man sinned, or his parents, but that the works of God might be made manifest in him." (John 9:1-3)

2. "Do not be deceived, God is not mocked: for whatever a man sows, that he will also reap." (Galatians 6:7)
3. "He who leads into captivity shall go into captivity; he who kills with the sword must be killed with the sword. Here is the patience and the faith of the saints." (Revelation 13:10)
4. "The point is this: He who sows sparingly will also reap sparingly; and he who sows bountifully will also reap bountifully." (II Corinthians 9:6)
5. "As you have done, it shall be done to you, your deeds shall return on your own head." (Obadiah 1:15)

Quoting again from Cranston & Williams concerning Karma as related to our current existence, "We are born an infant and inherit a body that could be healthy or diseased, handsome or ugly, well-developed or maimed. Why? What did we do to deserve this good or evil fortune? Simultaneously, we inherit parents (rich or poor, loving or indifferent), a nation, a time and geographical environment, a culture, and so on - all of which powerfully affect us. Now we are stuck with it and call it the accident of birth. Why were we not born in the Middle-Ages? Or in the jungles of South America, or among the war-ravaged, starving peoples of Vietnam or Cambodia?"

Professor Geddes MacGregor in his book Reincarnation in Christianity uses the analogy of a book, "Reincarnation takes care of the problem of moral injustice. To the age-old question of Job (Why do the wicked prosper and the righteous suffer?) the reincarnationist has a ready answer; we are seeing, in this life, only a fragment of a long story. If you come in at the chapter in which the villain beats the hero to a pulp, of course you will ask the old question. You may even put down the book at this point and join forces with those who call life absurd, seeing no justice in the universe. This is because you are too impatient to go on to hear the rest of the story, which will unfold a much richer pattern in which the punishment of the wicked and the vindication of the righteous will be brought to light. Death is but the end of a chapter; it is not, as the nihilists suppose, the end of the story."

Professor Huston Smith in his book *The Religions of Man* noted, "Science has alerted the Western world to the importance of causal relationships in the physical world. Every physical event has its cause, and every cause will have its determinate effects. India extends this concept of universal causation to include man's moral and spiritual life as well. To some extent the West has also. 'As a man sows, so shall he reap'; or again, 'Sow a thought and reap an act, sow an act and reap a habit, sow a habit and reap a character, sow a character and reap a destiny' - these are ways the West has put the point. The difference is that India tightens up and extends its concept of moral law to see it as absolutely binding and brooking no exceptions."

"The present condition of each individual's interior life - how happy he is, how confused or serene, how much he can comprehend - is an exact product of what he has wanted and got in the past; and equally, his present thoughts and decisions are determining his future states. Each act he directs upon the world has its equal and opposite reaction on himself. Each thought and deed delivers an unseen chisel blow toward the sculpturing of his destiny."

Most who study the Edgar Cayce readings accept that every individual in the world is a "spiritual being having a human experience" on earth, living in a sequence of lifetimes (reincarnation) designed to provide ample opportunities to awaken spiritually and achieve a sense of oneness with God and fellow beings.

Following is that philosophy as described by a poet:

> I hold that when a person dies
> His soul returns again to Earth;
> Arrayed in some new flesh-disguise,
> Another mother gives him birth,
> With sturdier limbs and brighter brain,
> The old soul takes the road again.
> *John Mansfield*

It is reasonable to accept that people living in this current age also participated in the biblical events as recorded. Of the 2,500 Cayce life readings, about 500 were for individuals who lived in Old Testament times. Now flesh and blood may not inherit eternal life; only the Spirit, only the purpose, only the desire may inherit same.

Lest individuals think they have unlimited lifetimes to overcome karmic habits, Cranston and Williams in their book on *Reincarnation* noted that Christ warned that there is a time limit for attainment of perfection and said, "When the number of the perfect souls shall be at hand, I will shut the gates of light and no one from that time onwards will enter in nor will anyone hereafter go forth (reincarnate) for the number of the perfect souls is completed, for the sake of which the universe has arisen."

There is considerable mystical doctrine that heaven consists of seven different levels of spiritual attainment - thus the oft quoted phrase of "Seventh Heaven". To pursue this further, I have invented the term "Karmic-Bouyancy" to reflect your spiritual level upon death and how you will be judged as to your Karmic journey into the various levels of spiritual attainment.

Dr. Ian Stevenson, Carlson Professor of Psychiatry who spent much of his life investigating the veracity of some 1700 cases of people (both adults & children) who seemed to have memories of prior lives. He has published several volumes of case histories, traveled extensively to verify their accuracy and discovered 90% to be accurate.

Helena Petrovna Blavatsky, a Russian noblewoman who studied in India & Tibet and was a principal founder of the Theosophical movement. She published a book entitled "Key to Theosophy" which is regarded as the "Textbook" on Metemphycosis (Reincarnation)

Similar to Helena Blavatsky, another viewpoint on the Theosophical movement comes from India where reincarnation has been an inherent belief. It comes from a publication entitled, "The Ancient Wisdom" by author Annie Besant & published by "The Theosophical Publishing House" in India. The author discusses the various planes of existence and I quote from her book:

A. The Physical Plane; "Man by his thoughts strikes the keynote of his music, and sets up the rhythms that are the most powerful factors in the continual changes in his physical and spiritual bodies". In sleep, although consciousness leaves the physical body the etheric body remains intertwined. However, in death both the consciousness and the etheric body separate from the physical body.

B. The Astral Plane; "The spirit-matter of the astral plane exists in seven subdivisions, as we have seen in the spirit-matter of the physical plane. An astral entity can change his whole appearance with startling rapidity, taking on form under every impulse of thought".

C. Kamaloka (Purgatory); "Literally the place or habitat of desire (a part of the Astral Plane) where the etheric body is absorbed in the contemplation of the panorama of his past life, which in the death hour un-roles before him, complete in every detail. (The book of life revealed). Eventually, all souls in this astral plane (except for a degraded, small, minority) shake off the bonds of the astral body and awaken to the bliss of the heaven world".

D. The Mental Plane; "The word Man comes from the Sanskrit verb, to think, so that Man means the Thinker, he is named by his most characteristic attribute, intelligence. This individual is Manas, or the thinker, he is the self, clothed in matter – he reveals his presence on the physical plane by the vibrations he sets up in the brain and nervous system. According to the stage of evolution reached by the man will be the type of mental body he forms in this life. There are three types of men; an undeveloped man, an average man & a spiritually advanced man. The growth of the permanent body which, with the divine consciousness, forms the Thinker is extremely slow. Its technical name is the causal body, because he gathers up the results of all experiences, and these act as causes, molding future lives".

E. Devachan (Heaven); "The total length of time spent here depends upon ones Karmic condition in this past life. We will now study the seven subdivisions of Devchan, remembering that in the four lower levels we were in a world of form, and a world, moreover, in which every thought presents itself at once as a form:

1. The first region is a heaven of least progressed souls whose highest emotion on earth was a narrow, sincere and sometimes unselfish love for family & friends.

2. The second region comprises men and women of every religious faith whose hearts during their earthly lives had turned with loving devotion to God, under any name.

3. The third region is composed of beings who were devoted servants of humanity while on earth.

4. The fourth region is composed of advanced souls adept in the arts, music, nature and students of religious philosophy.

5.   The fifth region is for souls who during their earth-life were deep thinkers and noble persons, who have sown much seed.
6.   In the sixth heaven are more advanced souls, who during earth life had felt but little attraction for its passing shows, and who devoted all their energies to the higher intellectual and moral life.
7.   In the seventh heaven, yet higher, lovelier, here the masters and initiates have their intellectual home.

Edgar Cayce, a 20th century American clairvoyant & healer who had the ability to assess the Akashic record of individuals to divulge their past lives. Otherwise known as the Book of Life.

Other views of some of the great historical figures on the subject of reincarnation:

1.   Henry Ford as a young man wondered why we were born and asked, "What are we here for?" Subsequently he was given a book on reincarnation which changed his entire life, purpose & meaning. His contribution to society needs no further comment except that he received intuitively the process of mass producing the automobile.
2.   Charles Lindbergh whose book, The Spirit of St. Louis, was preceded by his initial story "We" because he was accompanied on his solo flight by spiritual friends who controlled his flight path whenever he fell asleep.
3.   Thomas Edison whose prolific inventions changed the world – he could take short naps and intuitively knew the next steps for each invention.

One of the Cayce phrases that provides the essence of this chapter is, "Spirit is the life, Mind is the builder, the Physical is the result" In other words, Spirit gives us the life force, It's with our mind that we pattern it and the physical is the result.

Chapter V

The Greatest Stories Never Told

Christian tradition teaches only the New Testament version of "Jesus the Christ" as the only historical appearance of this "Master Soul" – although in this very gospel, "He stated that he was the *First Adam & The Last Adam*".

Psychic sources who are able access the Akashic-Records tell a more fascinating story about God's First Begotten Son and his involvement with the first Homo-Sapiens – some 300,000 years ago. Edgar Cayce had this ability while in trance to access the Akashic-Records for individuals as well as global events.

Before God initiated the "Big Bang" which subsequently produced all the stars in heaven as well as our solar system, he created his "First Begotten Son, the Word" or "The Master Soul" (The Christ Spirit) and in concert with God they created trillions of companion spirit entities (you & me) – all were given the gift of free-will.

In addition, God created a spiritual network of Angels & Archangels who formed his governing cabinet (Intranet) to carry out His various directives.

After our Earth was created and had cooled enough to support various life forms – animal, vegetable & mineral – the earth became a veritable "Jurassic Park". This attracted the attention of many of the Companion Spirit Entities who became enamored with the variety & habits of these creations. Since these spirit entities were given the gift of free will, many elected to penetrate the physical bodies of various life forms and to enjoy their habits and would enter & leave at will. Unfortunately, some overstayed and became entrapped. As a result, they and their offspring became mixtures and in the early chapters of Genesis in the "Old Testament" became known as the "Sons & Daughters of Men.

This concerned the Master Soul who descended into the earth plane in astral form to try to rescue these hapless souls, some 300,000 years ago, who resided on the continent of Lemuria. He was known as Amelius and remained in astral form while he created a new root race known today as the Brown race (also known as part of the third root race). Some of them followed the Only One God teachings of Amelius but others created their own idols and as a result, some 80,000 years later, the continent of Lemuria broke up and became completely submerged with some occupants fleeing to what is now South America and the Southwestern United States and others to the Mid-Eastern areas such as India.

These third root races were created by the will of God along with the Master Soul with a sturdy upright stance and a larger brain that could differentiate between "Good & Evil".

The Master Soul (Amelius) now became the *"First Adam"* and began a series of incarnate lives (some thirty according to Cayce & the Akashic-Records) as recorded in the Judeo-Christian bibles.

Following are the greatest stories, never before told, that identifies most of the Master Soul's incarnations from Adam to Christ:

The Genealogy of Jesus Christ

Contemporary theologians including Pope John Paul II, refer to Jesus (Christ) as the first Adam and on the order of Melchizedek. Various seers & mystics including Edgar Cayce indicate that Jesus (Christ) was indeed a reincarnation of the first Adam.

The readings of Edgar Cayce indicate that the Jesus Soul (Christ Spirit) may have lived as many as thirty different lives and he clearly identifies the following (henceforth these incarnations will be italicized).

Amelius - an incarnation in spirit form only and was the first soul created or begotten by God.

Adam - the first Son of God (Homo Sapien) described in the opening of the Bible (Genesis).

In the Edgar Cayce readings there were many references to the first Adam, e.g., "When there was in the beginning a man's advent into the plane known as earth and it became a living soul, amenable to the laws that govern the plane itself as presented, the Son of God, the Son of the First Cause, making manifest in the material body." Also, "He, that Christ Consciousness, is that first spoken of in the beginning when God said, "Let there be light, and there was light. And that is the light manifested in the Christ. First, it became physically conscious in Adam. And as in Adam we all die, so in the last Adam – Jesus becoming the Christ – we are all made alive". And finally, "For, know that He who was lifted up on the Cross in Calvary – was …also he that first walked among men at the beginning of man's advent into flesh! For He indeed was and is the first Adam, the last Adam; that is the way, the truth, the light!

The fifteenth chapter of 1st – Corinthians, Verse 22 states "For as in Adam all die, so also in Christ shall all be made alive" and in verse 45, "Thus it is written, the first man Adam became a living being, the last Adam became a life-giving spirit".

In the book "Lives of the Master", author Glenn Sanderfur quotes Adam's son Seth in the 'Testament of Adam – "And I, Seth, wrote this testament. And my Father died, and they buried him at the East of Paradise opposite the first city built on the earth. And Adam was borne to his grave by the Angels and Powers of heaven because he had been created in the image of God. And the sun and moon were darkened, and there was thick darkness for seven days. And we sealed this testament and we put it in the cave of treasures with the offerings Adam had taken out of Paradise, gold and myrrh and frankincense. And the sons of kings, the magi will come and get them, and they will take them to the Son of God, to Bethlehem of Judea, to the cave." This was from the book "Life of Adam and Eve" circulating around 100 BC.

Enoch – the book of Jude (verses 14-15) refers to him, "It was of these also that Enoch in the seventh generation from Adam prophesied, saying, "Behold, the Lord came with His holy myriads, to execute judgment on all, and to convict all the ungodly of all their deeds of ungodliness which they have committed in such an ungodly way, and of the harsh things which ungodly sinners have spoken against Him"

Enochian authority, Dr. R.H. Charles notes that the influence of Enoch on the New Testament was greater than all other apocryphal and pseudo-graphical books taken together. The "Ethiopan Book of Enoch" was considered to have been Paul's constant reference book, John was also influenced by Enoch as was Peter in his letters.

Enoch was known as the Scribe of Righteousness. Cayce considered him responsible for writing much of the Old Testament. There is strong evidence that Enoch and Hermes of Egypt were the same person. Hermes was considered to be the architect of the Great Pyramid around 10,500 BC. He was also known as the "Scribe of Gods" and "Lord of Divine words."

The Jewish Kabbalah relates that Enoch (Hermes) constructed underground vaults to preserve the secret teachings received by Seth from Adam. This is confirmed by Cayce who indicates these vaults are located under the Great Pyramid and there are copies in sealed vaults under the remains of Atlantis.

Melchizedek – In the Old Testament story of Abraham (Genesis 14:18-20) it reads "And Melchizedek, king of Salem, brought out bread and wine, for he was priest of God Most High, and he blessed Abram and said, "Blessed be Abram by God Most High, who has delivered your enemies into your hand! And Melchizedek changed Abram's name to Abraham who in turn gave Melchizedek a tenth of everything he owned." The Canon of the Catholic Church credits Melchizedek with the practice of tithing which was adopted by most Christian religions.

In the New Testament (Hebrews 7:3) it refers to Melchizedek as, "Without (human) father, or mother or genealogy, and has neither beginning of days, nor end of life, but resembling the son of God he continues a priest forever."

Birger A. Pearson after studying the Nag Hammadi Library (ancient documents that were discovered in the late 1940s) noted, "We are drawn to the conclusion that, in the revelation which the priest Melchizedek has received, he has seen that he himself will have a redemptive role to play as the suffering, dying, resurrected Savior, Jesus Christ!"

Cayce intimated that Melchizedek is the author of the book of Job and also that his teachings were instrumental in the formation of the School of Prophets in the Essene Community.

Joseph- The eleventh son of Jacob who was the subject of an earlier prophecy in Numbers 24.17 which foretold, "I see him, but not now; I behold him, but not at night; a star shall come forth out of Jacob, and a scepter shall rise out of Israel". -----Although Jacob had ten prior children, Joseph was the first born to his favorite wife Rachel and Joseph became the favorite son. We all know the subsequent story of Joseph being sold into slavery by his jealous brothers and his eventual promotion as second in command to the Pharoah. Most scholars agree that Joseph's stay in Egypt was between 1720 BC and 1550 BC – or about 400 years before Moses.

There are some interesting comparisons between the story of Joseph and Jesus as related in the Cayce readings:

1. Joseph was sold for 20 pieces of silver by his brother Judah, and Jesus was sold for 30 pieces of silver by his disciple Judas. Jewish historian Josephus claims that the actual amount paid for Joseph was also 30 pieces of silver.
2. Joseph spent three years in an Egyptian prison before his remarkable promotion to Pharoah's court and Jesus spent three days in the grave before his remarkable resurrection.
3. The lives of both Joseph and Jesus were saved by going to Egypt. Joseph's brothers would have killed him and Jesus, as a baby would have been killed by Herod's decree.
4. Joseph began his career at the age of thirty and Jesus began his ministry at the age of thirty.
5. Both Joseph and Jesus were rejected by their own people but exalted by foreigners. Joseph exalted by the Egyptians and Jesus by the Gentiles.

In the "Testament of Joseph" he made the following prophecy, "And I saw that from Judah was born a virgin wearing a linen garment, and from her was born a lamb, without spot, and all the beasts rushed against him, and the lamb overcame them and trod them under foot. And because of him the angels and men rejoiced and all the land. And these things shall come to pass in their season, in the last days."

According to Cayce, "During the forty years in the wilderness, the children of Israel carried Joseph's body with them, although no mention is made of those who had the responsibility for caring for it. This was four centuries after Joseph's death."

Joshua –In those days when Moses was involved in delivering the Israelites from Egyptian bondage, Joshua was a member of the "Chosen People" and became an important minister to Moses. He also represented his tribe, Ephraim, and was Moses's interpreter with the people. After the forty years wandering in the desert and after Moses's death, he was chosen by God to lead the Israelites to the Promised Land.

Cayce noted that Joshua inherited a very disciplined nation that had been spiritually cleansed during their forty years in the wilderness. Prior to that time they had practiced many forms of self-indulgence and Moses introduced strict prohibitions on these activities, which included sodomy, incest, homosexuality, child sacrifice, stealing, lying, cannibalism, child-prostitution and other injustices. His ten commandments were aimed at controlling these temptations.

Cayce had an interesting observation concerning Joshua, "Four-hundred-year cycles play a recurrent part in the spiritual history of Israel. When the book of Exodus opens, the four-hundred year of captivity foretold to Abraham is nearly completed. Four centuries have passed between the death of Joseph and this soul's rebirth as Joshua. An identical time span occurs between this last Old Testament incarnation and his reincarnation as Jeshua, the high priest at the time of the rebuilding of Jerusalem".

Upon entering the Promised Land the ritual of circumcision was again promulgated and became a permanent rite for the Jewish people. This was also the time when the city of Jericho fell when Joshua had his army circle the city seven times for seven days and a final trumpet blast along with shouting caused the walls to crumble.

Joshua's conquest of the Promised Land began with the crossing of the Jordan River. Jesus's ministry began with his baptism in the Jordan River. Tradition has it that both incidents occurred at the exact spot. This is also the spot where Adam is supposed to have begun his exiled life from Eden by standing in the Jordan River.

God commanded Joshua to eliminate the pagan remnants of the pre-Adamic (Son's of Men), creations who then populated the "Promised Land". These included the giants of that day who were the result of genetically increasing size & strength without spiritual awareness or mental ability. As these remnants were eliminated, their souls would be forced to reincarnate into Adamic bodies thus expediting their return to God's purpose.

According to Cayce, Joshua was responsible for documenting the first five books of the Old Testament (the Torah). In his final days Joshua warned the people to keep the faith or they would lose their land and he said, "There is set before you good and evil, life and death, choose thou this day whom you will serve. As for me and my house, we will serve the Living God." Joshua died at the age of 110 years and was buried on Mount Ephraim.

Asaph - during the reign of King David, Asaph was the court musician and psalmist as well as the king's interpreter to the people. He was also a key figure in the new Temple built by King Solomon at a later date. In addition to the duties mentioned, he was the King's seer and he prophecyised in speech and verse. He was the author of biblical psalms 50 and 73 through 83. There is even speculation that Asaph's writings may have been the basis for Aesop's fables.

Zend –The Cayce readings state that Zend was the father of Zoroaster and Zend was an incarnation of the Master Soul who lived in the period of Darius who succeeded his father Cyrus the great (who then freed the Israelites from bondage by the Babylonians and earlier permitted Jeshua to return them all to Jerusalem and begin rebuilding their temple). It appears Zend lived in the period around 485 B.C. and his father was named Uhjltd (interestingly in some of Cayce's readings he (Cayce) was this same person in a prior life).

Zend's son was born in this same period who became a great prophet, his name was Zarathrustra (Greek name Zoroaster). Recently, the USA helped in saving followers of Zoroaster in Syria to escape certain death at the hands of Islamic terrorists. They are known as the Yasidi sect.

Jesus - needs no introduction and who became the ***Christ***. Our biblical literature (New Testament) covers his early childhood and his ministry after age 30, with little detail about His life in between. Cayce said Jesus spent these intervening years studying and traveling. He traveled back to Egypt (Hermes), then to India (Buddhists) and also to Persia (Magi) - underlining the universality of all enlightened religions.

It is particularly significant that at the birth of Jesus he was visited by the "Wise Men" (Magi) who brought the ritual elements of gold, myrrh & frankincense that were mentioned in the "Testament of Adam" previously.

However, there is another story about the women involved in the Master's life both before his birth and before he began his ministry. Cayce said it began at the School of the Prophets that was established by Elijah at Mt. Carmel (known as the Essenes which means "Expectancy" whose purpose was to prepare a young woman to become a suitable channel for the future birth of highly evolved souls and with the expectancy that one of them would someday be the mother of the Messiah).

Accordingly, Cayce offers the following story about Mary's selection as the mother of Jesus, "When Mary was 13-years old along with 11 other maidens they were going at sunrise to the temple to offer prayers and burn incense. As Mary reached the top step, an angel appeared and took her by the hand, to become the chosen one". Among her companions were Andra, Edithia and Josie who would all play roles in the life of Jesus. When the Holy Family fled to Egypt to escape Herod's attempt to kill all children in the kingdom under the age of two (to preempt the disclosure of the Magi that Jesus was to become the "King of the Jews") it was Josie that accompanied them and became their handmaiden as well as a teacher to the young Jesus.

Another woman was Edithia whose father Apsafar was the innkeeper in Bethlehem who said there was "no room in the inn". He was also a member of the Essenes and was trying to protect Mary & Joseph from the rabble. Apsafar's wife along with Edithia assisted in the birth of Jesus. Cayce said that Mary was 16 when she gave birth.

Among the Essenes, women were highly revered and many of their leaders were women. Judy was not only a leader among the Essenes but a prophet and healer as well. She was the one who selected Josie to accompany the Holy Family when they fled to Egypt. She became the primary teacher of Jesus when he became more mature, she was instrumental in encouraging Him to visit India, Persia and Egypt before He, began His ministry.

Martha was the wife of Nicodemus (who was a member of the Sandhedrin who ruled the synagogue and feared that Jesus would try to destroy their power). She was a dedicated follower of Jesus and being an expert at weaving. She made a special robe for Jesus which Cayce explained was, "woven in one piece with a hole in the top for his head and a body with cords to bound about the waist. The color of the robe was pearl gray with Jewish symbols woven in at the bottom". She was with Mary at the foot of the Cross when Jesus was executed and witnessed the Roman soldiers casting lots for His robe.

The other woman who played a role in Jesus's life was Mary Magdalene who Cayce said "was of Grecian and Jewish descent, about 5-feet 4-inches tall, weighing 121 pounds with, hair almost red, and blue eyes". She was a courtesan to wealthy Romans until the fateful day when the Master saved her from stoning and at the age of 23 she was cleansed by Jesus of "avarice, hate, self-indulgence and those of the kindred selfishness; hopelessness and blasphemy" and she became one of His most devoted disciples.

So it can be said that many women were also disciples of Jesus.

In Harvey E. Elliott's "The Origin of Religions", he revealed some of the missing links in the biography of Jesus obtained from ancillary religious writings:

At an early age, He was placed by the Essenes, in the charge of the keepers of the Monastery and School of Mount Carmel, with instructions as to his education. This school was maintained by three organizations - the Nazarites, the Nazarenes and the Essenes.

Christ, It appears, was registered at Mt. Carmel, which was commonly known as the school of the prophets, under the name of Joseph.

He graduated from that school at the age of thirteen, at which time He, was placed under the care of two Magi who took him to a school in what **is** now known as Puri, on the East Coast of India. This trip, it is said, consumed an entire year. It appears He spent over a year in the Monastery at Puri and that his principle instructor was named Lamaas.

From Puri He went to Benares where for a period He studied the Hindu method of healing under the Master named Udraki, reputed to have been the ablest in India. After this, it is said, He spent considerable time visiting different parts of India and then returned to Puri for another period of two years after which He spent a short period teaching in a little town called Katck.

On leaving Katck, it appears Christ went to Persia, where He studied at Persepolis, the ancient palace of the <u>King of Kings</u>, burned by Alexander in 321 B.C.

From Greece He went directly to Heliopolis, Egypt, where later He received his Master's degree in the Great Pyramid.

In considering what the bible has to say about the teachings of Jesus, Edouard Schure in his book "From Sphinx to Christ" referred to the value of the four Gospels, "It is acknowledged that the Greek Gospels were written long after the death of Jesus, and based upon Jewish traditions which could be traced back to the disciples and eyewitnesses of the Master's life. Whether or not they contain certain contradictions of detail, and present the prophet of Galilee from different angles, in what does the authority and truth of these writings consist for us? Is it in the date of their composition? Is it in the mountains of commentaries that have been heaped upon them? No. Their force and their truth depend upon the living unity of the person and teaching of Jesus which they reveal, and we have for counterproofs the fact that this revelation has changed the face of the world, and the new life that it can still arouse in each one of us."

Rudolph Steiner corroborates the validity of the four Gospels, "Modern criticism of the Gospels throws light only upon the outer and material side of these documents. It teaches us nothing concerning their essence. So great a personality as that of the Christ could not be comprehended by any one of His disciples. He must have shown a different side of His Nature to each of them, according to their faculties. If we take a photograph of a tree from one side only, we have but a partial likeness; but if we took it from four different sides, the likeness is complete".

Edouard Schure complements Steiner's observation with, "It is the same with the Gospels. Each of them corresponds to a different degree of initiation, and presents to us a different side of the nature of Jesus Christ. Matthew and Luke depict in preference the Master Jesus, that is to say, the human nature of the founder of Christianity. Mark and John describe chiefly His divine and spiritual nature".

Lytle Robinson in "Edgar Cayce's Story of the Origin and Destiny of Man" noted, "The Great Pyramid of Gizeh stands as an historical monument to the present root race. It records the story of man's struggle for spiritual wisdom, and for many ages it was used as a temple of initiation for the world's great teachers and leaders. It was finally in there that the Great Initiate, Jesus, who became the Christ, took the final initiate degrees, along with John the Baptist, His forerunner".

In His ministry He reaffirmed His direct relationship with God and, John Paul II in his book "Crossing the Threshold of Hope" addressed this point, "Even the day before the Passion the apostles asked Christ: 'Show us the Father'. His response remains fundamental: "How can you say, Show us the Father? Do you not believe that I am in the Father and the Father in me...Or else, believe because of the works themselves.....The Father and I are one"

Edouard Schure in the aforementioned publication expanded on the Christ Phenomenon; "In the Christ there appeared for the first time a God Completely incarnated in humanity. This phenomenon could only happen once in history, at the critical moment of human evolution - that is, at the lowest point of its descent into matter. How was it to rise again from this darkness to the heights of the Spirit? Only through the great impetus given by a God who was made man - and, this impetus once given, the Word would still continue to act upon and influence humanity, though actual incarnation would not again be necessary".

"Hence the marvelous organism of the Being called Jesus Christ. Through His sensations, He is in and of matter through His thoughts He soars to the world of Archetypes. He breathes divinity. His whole consciousness is expressed in the words so often on His lips: 'I and the father are one'. At the same time He is one with suffering humanity through one all-embracing tenderness, the great Love, which caused Him voluntarily to accept His mission.........His thoughts do not stumble through the slippery lanes of reason; they flash forth from the central Truth that embraces all things......The object of His mission is the spiritualisation of the world and of man, the raising of them to a higher level of evolution. The means used are both moral and intellectual - moral, through love and the feeling of universal brotherhood which flow from Him as from an inexhaustible spring; intellectual and spiritual through the opening of the Mysteries to all souls who are athirst for truth."

"Thus during His three years ministry, the Christ initiates the community into His moral teachings and the apostles into those ancient Mysteries which He revives and expands. But, in contrast to what happened formerly in Persia, Egypt, Greece and Judea, this initiation, then reserved for a chosen few only, now took place publicly and in broad daylight, that the whole of humanity might participate."

Jesus wanted to prepare His three chosen disciples to carry on His mission in the world after His departure as noted in the account of St. Matthew, "And after six days Jesus takes Peter, James and John his brother and brings them up into a high mountain apart, and was transfigured before them; and his face did shine as the sun, and his raiment was white as the light."

Cayce described the three primary appearances of Jesus; Adam, Enoch, and Melchezidek - as "in the perfection" and distinguished them from the later ones which were "in the earth"- Joseph, Joshua, Jeshua. And Jesus, in His resurrected body is "without days or years and once again High Priest "after the order of Melchezedek."

Robert Krajenke, commenting on Cayce's biblical dissertations, noted, "Following The Book of Ruth, the Old Testament begins to center chiefly on the family of David. Boaz was part Canaanite (descended from Rahab of Jericho, Joshua 2:1). Ruth was a Moabite. Outside blood then, was an integral part of the chosen family of a chosen nation. As David is viewed by Christians as a foreshadowing of "The kingship of Christ Jesus". This blood mixture is also seen as representing Christ's authority over all nations."

Rodney Stark writing in the March/April 1998 issue of A.R.E. publication "Venture Inward" noted that, "Between A.D. 60 and A.D. 100, the number of Christians increased from a meager 3,000 to 7,500 and to more than 40,000 by the year A.D. 150. By the year A.D. 200, the total would exceed 200,000 then climb to 1,000,000 by A.D. 250 soar to an astonishing 6,000,000 by the turn of the century or 10% of the Roman Empire's entire population." After Emperor Constantine, he continued, "By A.D. 350, rolls of the empire's Christians had reached 33,000,000 or half the populace, and their consortiums of burgeoning Churches would one day surpass Rome's legions in dominion & sweep".

At the Pentecost where Peter gave the sermon and everyone in the large crowd from many countries heard his sermon in their own language; then began the selection of Apostles who were to travel around the known world to spread the Gospel ("Good News"). Following are the initial assignments for these specific Apostles:

1. John – would travel first to Ephesus.
2. Peter – would travel to Rome
3. Paul – would travel first to Ephesus & then to Rome
4. Andrew – would travel to Achaea, Patrae & Caesarea
5. Thomas – would travel to India

Finally, John White, a contributing writer for Venture Inward in the November/December 2006 issue of Venture Inward summarizes the current day status of Christianity and the search for the Holy Grail. He reflects on the fact that Christ did not teach Christianity but taught self-liberation or God-realization. However, today the religion of Jesus has become a religion primarily about Jesus or a cult of personality rather than a path for self-transcendence. He goes on to say that it has become Churchianity, whose primary objective is the ego-driven maintenance of power, authority and wealth. In the process, mainstream Christian thought changed from the mystical-metaphysical teaching of Jesus to the magical-mythical teaching of church officials.

There has been an ongoing effort to find relics of saints that that can become important for Church member meditation and for use in new church structures. However, the 12th century search for a relic of Christ himself became a search for the Holy Grail or the burial cloth of Jesus Christ. In the year 1307 AD a search began in earnest to find this Holy Grail (The Shroud of Christ). The Knights Templar from the Temple of Solomon found the Shroud and it was secretly stored in a wooden box with an opening that allowed the face of a bearded man to be viewed as a form of worship. It is currently located in the Cathedral of St. John the Baptist at Turin, Italy and has undergone rigorous scientific testing to assure its authenticity. New chemical testing find the Shroud dates back to the first century AD. They have also identified pollen grains on the Shroud that could only have come from the vicinity of Jerusalem. And blood stains from the Shroud are real and type AB and contain human male DNA. For more information on the Shroud go to the Shroud of Turin Website, www.shroud.com based in Los Angeles.

We have not mentioned the life of the Buddha, who was born in the 6th century BC. His father, Suddhodana, was the king in a section of India that was located between the Himalayan mountains and the river Rohini. Along the mountain bases several ascetic monks lived quietly and separately and in constant meditation.

His father named him Siddartha, and summoned the most famous of the ascetics to predict the future of Siddartha, since his father expected him to become a famous warrior and would someday replace him.

The ascetic said he would become a great spiritual leader and that his mother was a virgin at conception and that his mother would die shortly since she was born only for this purpose. Also, that Siddartha would become this great leader after three things happened in his life, first he would see an old, decrepit subject of the king and would ask, what happened that this person could become so old and he received no good answer, secondly he would see a dead person along the road, again he did not receive a satisfactory why and finally (when in disguise) he saw how poor & neglected the entire population was.

To prevent this from happening when Siddartha was older, his father ordered the most beautiful young girls in his kingdom to come to the castle for his son's coming out party and in accordance with custom he married and they had a child named Rahula. The king built them a private residence and ordered his servants to keep fresh flowers, music and entertainment at all times so that Siddartha and his bride would have a luxurious & happy life with nothing to remind them of the predictions of the ascetic.

Then Siddartha asked his servant guard to take him outside the palace to see what the world was like – and subsequently the ascetic's predictions became true. He was unable to shake these terrible memories and he resolved to renounce his crown and leave the palace and his family to dedicate himself to an ascetic life.

Siddartha changed his name to Gotama, an historical family name of Vedic singers, and at the age of twenty-nine years he left the palace & his family to seek deliverance in solitude and truth in meditation. (How parallel to Jesus's birth and starting his ministry at age 30).

Gotama now became a wanderer, yellow-robed, and with shaven head, a beggar through the villages, wooden bowl in hand. He sought out the highest Brahmans asking for the way to truth; but their abstract & complicated statements did not satisfy him and he resolved to seek the truth through his own strength and solitary meditation.

He eventually became the enlightened one with long hair & beard and left his meditation abode to begin his preaching at Benares. He first converted five monks who became his fervent disciples. His aura field became widespread and crowds soon followed him, pupils left their masters for him. Kings & queens arrived mounted on elephants and offered him homage and friendship and many converted as well. His own father, son & wife bowed down to him and became followers.

Tradition has preserved his sermon at Benares, which is Buddha's Sermon on the Mount:

"You call me friend, but you do not give me my true name. I am the Delivered One, the Blessed One, the Buddha. Open your ears. Deliverance from death has been found. You will recognize the truth. Not mortification, but renunciation of the pleasures of the senses. This Eight-fold path is called: Right Doctrine, Right Purpose, Right Discourse, Right Action, Right Living, Right Aspiration, Right Thought, Right Meditation. This Oh monks, is the sacred truth concerning the cessation of suffering: it is the lust for life, from rebirth to rebirth, the lust for pleasure, for becoming, for power. The suppression of lust by the destruction of desire – putting it outside of one's self, freeing one's self from it, leaving no place for it.

It is this doctrine that drives Buddhist families to turn over their small male children to the Buddhist religious enclaves in the hope they will be spared the rebirth cycle. Unfortunately, this may not be the entire solution if the child's Karma requires more resolution. However, the Buddhists are very peaceful by nature with very low crime rates or other societal problems.

Chapter VI

In Retrospect

As we review the mystical explanations of Genesis Revisited (Chapter I), answers to some perplexing questions emerge from the mist. Certainly it is clear that we are spiritual beings first and foremost (with a soul) but currently living in a material body. We understand a little better whence we have come and why. Yes, there is life after death!

We must also conclude that souls continue to reincarnate into new fetuses, probably at the time of the "quickening", and are certainly fully incarnated at the first breath. Also, parents are chosen based upon "like attracts like" and karmic lessons to be learned by all parties.

A recent Watchtower tract entitled "Hope for the Dead" insists that when a person dies he is dead until resurrection day and these Jehovah's Witnesses are not alone in this belief. The tract goes on to state that man does not have an immortal soul which is contrary to all that we have just learned. They base their conclusion on a literal interpretation of their Bible.

Cayce commented upon Biblical interpretations, "Almost all portions of Scripture can be interpreted on three levels: literal, metaphysical, and spiritual. But for any level to be valid, it must be practical and applicable and able to be coordinated with the other levels and be as one, even as the Father, Son and Holy Spirit are one.

The "Fall" or "Original Sin" is more understandable when we hear the "Fire & Brimstone" preachers tell us "We are all sinners!" Obviously, sin is putting material desires ahead of spiritual desires and the Bible is a history of these personal battles, accumulating good Karma or bad Karma in each lifetime.

Robert W. Krajenke noted Cayce's view of these choices, "These two principles of spirit (Good & Evil) still exist, as they did in the beginning. A soul can choose consistently to eat from the Tree of life, and thus maintain his connection to the Source; or use his existence only to experience the things of the world in a manner which gives him knowledge, yet results in separation and eventual death of the Spirit within".

Which religion is the right religion should be viewed from the standpoint of their creed, dogma (Canon) and social acceptance. Your specific choice has more to do with family custom than with spiritual achievements. Most importantly, it is your spiritual ideals that will best serve your religious goals.

S. Ralph Harlow in his book "A Life After Death" records a conversation with Arthur Ford's spiritual guide, Fletcher, concerning religion & spirituality in which Fletcher replies, "Over here we make a distinction between religion & spirituality. Many persons who are formally religious are not necessarily spiritual, and many who do not seem connected with formal religion are deeply spiritual. Race is not geographical and religion is universal".

In pursuing psychic experiences related in the Bible, Harlow states, "Surely no one can read the Epistles of St. Paul or the Book of Acts, which tell of St. Paul's conversion (long after Jesus's final ascension into Heaven) without admitting that here we have reports of psychic experiences. No other man had such influence on the spread of Christianity as did Paul. A trained religious leader among the Jews, a fanatical persecutor of the early Christians, he became the first great missionary of this faith he had persecuted, and a martyr for the Christ he once hated. Harlow goes on to say, "Here is psychic experience that was to shape all history, the importance of which cannot be overestimated. It transformed Saul of Tarsus, educated as a rabbi, into Paul the Missionary – a witness to the truth and universal nature of the Christian gospel.

Jesus the Christ initiated His "New Covenant" and expressed the terms and conditions for salvation in simple and elegant pronouncements:

"I am the way and the truth and the light, no one comes unto to the Father except through me"

When asked, what is the greatest commandment? He replied, "To love God with all your heart, your mind, and your soul and your neighbor as yourself"

"As a man thinks, so is he" (Thoughts are Things).

When Jesus was asked by His Disciples, "How shall we pray? Jesus taught them the Lord's Prayer which is used today by all Christian religions. Following is this prayer with added comments:

"Our Father which art in Heaven, Hallowed be His name" (Here Jesus wanted us to love God with all our hearts, all our minds and all our souls which is part of his most important commandment)

"Give us this day our daily bread" (Not only physical sustenance but spirit sustenance as well)

"Forgive us our trespasses as we forgive our trespassers" (The Law of Grace demands a forgiving nature and relates again to His most important commandment, "To love thy neighbor as thyself"

"Lead us not into temptation but deliver us from evil" (Help us to avoid material desires (sin) or bad Karma).

Now what do we do with the Moslem faith in this day & age with their infighting and the increase in radical thought and actions that concern people of every good faith. As difficult as it may be, Christians, Jews, Moslems, Buddhists, Hindus and other religious groups all believe in the "one God concept", although they may call Him by different names. As the psalmist observed (Psalm 139:7-10) "Whither shall I go from thy Spirit? Or whither shall I flee from thy presence? If I ascend up into heaven, thou art there. If I make my bed in hell, behold, thou art there. If I take the wings of the morning, and dwell in the uttermost parts of the seas; even there thy right hand holds me". Do we need the Crusaders again in the 21st century or can the moderate faiths join together to settle this ominous threat so that all can live in harmony?

Let us review the origin of Islam (Moslem religion) which was established by the prophet Mohammed in circa 622 AD when he and his older wife Khadija fled Mecca to the city of Yathrib, 220 miles North of Mecca. Mohammed said he was visited by the Archangel Gabriel who urged him to initiate a new religion based upon a new book called the Koran which Gabriel recited.

In Yathrib, Mohammed won quick success as religious leader and became governor of the city. In 630 AD he invaded Mecca in triumph and destroyed their many idols they worshipped and that were displayed in the Kaaba (cube) which also contained a large black meteorite – it eventually became the most sacred shrine of Islam and is located in Saudi Arabia. True believers are obligated to visit this sacred shrine at least once in their lifetime. In his earlier sermons, Mohammed emphasized that Christians, Jews and Moslems were all descendants of Abraham and therefore they were all brothers & sisters. Hopefully, Islam will remember this and decry the current highjack of Moslem leadership by evil forces that are intent on destroying everyone that does not agree with their extreme positions – whether they be Christian, Moslem or Jew.

Those Muslims who practice "Jihad" are influenced by Satanic forces and will be surprised after their physical death to find there are no 7-virgins and Allah is nowhere to be found. Instead they may spend hundreds of years in Purgatory facing their "Book of Life" which endlessly reveals their evil acts and when allowed to reincarnate must pay for these sins in their next lives.

In Chapter II we reviewed Darwin's treatise, "The Origin of the Species" where he purports that all living species developed from a single source that originated from the vast oceans. Unfortunately, his primary work concentrates on the vegetable part of "Animal, Vegetable & Mineral Species" with slight discourse on some winged species. His fellow anthropologists provided some criticisms but in many cases confirmed his basic theory and went further to conclude that this would include Man (Homo Sapiens).

Although Darwin never publically endorsed this conclusion. All atheists have adopted this view and many are in high level teaching positions and they have used their positions to insist that this should be the primary view being taught in all schools at all levels. Although Intelligent Design should certainly be taught as an alternate consideration. Another example of the dumbing down of our learning system in the USA.

Dr. Webb B. Garrison, author of <u>Strange Bonds Between Animals</u> and men, wrote, "Archeology has made great strides in the century since Darwin set the world agog. Mounting numbers of finds in Africa and Asia, as well as in Europe, have clarified the evolutionary paths of both men and apes. Today, no serious scientist supports the notion that humans are descendants of living anthropoid species. Most specialists now think that modern man, several extinct groups, and today's great apes are descendants from an unknown type of primate that thrived at least 30,000,000 years ago. Vague and scattered clues suggest that the family tree branched some 25,000,000 years ago. At least 500,000 years ago – perhaps earlier,-still obscure genetic changes led to the appearance of *Homo erectus*. Long extinct, this early human was followed by big-brained *Homo sapiens,* to which species belong all the races of men.

In Chapter III we discussed God's Intranet, the universal information network that provides the instincts and guidance to the Animal and Vegetable species through the Akashic-Field.

The aforementioned species do not have a soul as human's (Homo-Sapiens) possess, which gives them a direct connection to God through the Holy Spirit and when they were created they were given the gift of "Free Will" but expected to follow God's commandments faithfully. Many chose to remain in God's presence and became Angels and some Archangels. But the first-created by God became the Master Soul who was called God's first-born Son, the Mind, the Word and the Light who also became the "*Christ*" today.

Seven Archangels were created to become God's ruling cabinet, each with specific duties concerning the control of the Universe during and after its creation. One of them was named Lucifer, the Prince of Light, who before the Universe was created (before the Big-Bang), insisted that he be made equal with God which caused God to cast him & his subordinate followers into "Chaos" or the "Abyss". After the Universe was completed, with the Earth in its place, Lucifer and his followers, although remaining in spiritual form, entered the Earth plane and harassed God's followers. The negative versus the positive or evil versus good. When God finally created Man as a physical being, the battle of good versus evil became the norm.

Let us now look more closely at God's communication network, the Akashic-Field. I have selected Ervin Laszlo as my source for information concerning this amazing phenomena. He is the author of a book entitled, "Science and the Akashic Field". One of his colleagues wrote in the preface to this book, "Is every thing that ever happened on this earth recorded in some huge, ultra-dimensional information bank? Are some of us occasionally able to tap into it with some facility, and perhaps all of us to some extent now and then during our lives?". Laszlo provides the pioneering scientific answer to these and many other fundamental questions our species faces at this critical time in human evolution.

Laszlo, in one of his opening paragraphs sets the tone for his book by saying, "A particularly ambitious endeavor has surfaced in quantum physics in recent years: the attempt to create a Theory of Everything (a TOE). However, this goal of a single equation that could account for all the laws of the universe put forward so far are not theories of everything – they are at best theories of every physical thing. Life, mind and culture are part of the world's reality, and a genuine TOE would take them into account as well." In other words, the Akashic- Field. He goes on to say, "It makes sense to name the newly (re) discovered information field of the universe the A-Field. This A-Field takes its place among the fundamental fields of the universe, joining science's G-field (gravitational), EM field (electromagnetic) and the various nuclear and quantum fields. Life, mind, and culture are part of the world's reality and TOE would take them into account as well.

Regarding the chance that our earth is the only planet in the cosmos that contains life as we know it, consider Laszlo's scientific consideration, "Perhaps the most mysterious of all the cosmic puzzles is the fine tuning of the physical constants required to support life on our particular planet. There are some thirty factors involved with exceptional accuracy. For example, if the expansion rate of the early universe had been one-billionth less than it was, the universe would have collapsed almost immediately; and if it had been one-billionth more, it would have expanded so fast that it could only produce dilute, cold gases. Similarly, a small difference in the strength of the electromagnetic field relative to the gravitational field would have prevented the existence of hot and stable stars like our Sun. Similarly, if the difference between the mass of the neutron and proton were not precisely twice, no substantial chemical reaction could have taken place. And if the electric charge of electrons and protons did not balance precisely, all of matter would be unstable and consisting of nothing more than radiation and a mixture of gasses.

Laszlo also had some scientific solutions to the question, "Could our consciousness survive the physical demise of our body? It does not help to examine the human brain, for if consciousness continues to exist when brain function ceases, it is no longer associated with the brain. It is more to the point to look at evidence furnished by instances where consciousness is no longer linked with the brain. This is the case in near –death experiences (NDE'S). In such cases when the EEG is flat (certified death) and then they recover, they are able to recall in detailed events that occur during their resuscitation efforts."

Also, many people have experienced after-death communications with departed loved ones using competent mediums.

The search for Bridey Murphy was a sensational series in mass media that seemed to verify that reincarnation is a demonstrable fact, which was covered extensively in Chapter IV.

Let me add two pertinent quotes that summarize the elements of this document:

1. A poem whose author is unknown:

> Come, sail with me on a quiet Pond.
> We are the vessels on the Pond
> A fine wake spreads out behind us,
> We are interconnected parts of the whole,

Over and over the Cayce reading's insisted, "Be not deceived, God is not mocked. Whatsoever a man soweth, that shall he also reap". Ideals are dangerous and important business, the central business of every life. As Cayce repeated, "For no soul enters by chance"

Cayce in one of his readings said, "There are old souls and there are young souls. Some have grown spiritually, others have regressed. Some have had many experiences on earth to their credit; others few. But it has been according to their will of that individual, not God's. All those who have forgotten God have gradually been eliminated. Only souls that have reached a certain level of development have been permitted to incarnate"

I would like to conclude this treatise with an amazing impromptu trance reading by Edgar Cayce that confirms his ability to access the Akashic Record (Book of Life) and as well, how this record stores every event since the beginning of time. I quote as follows:

"This Psychic Reading was given by Edgar Cayce at the end of check-physical reading (1315-3), this 14th day of June, 1932, after suggestion was given three times for EC to wake up"

"PRESENT"

"Edgar Cayce; Gertrude Cayce, Conductor, Gladys Davis, Steno. Mildred Davis and Hugh Lynn Cayce."

"Reading"

"Time of reading – 11:30 A.M."

1. "EC: The Lords Supper – here with the Master – see what they had for supper – boiled fish, rice, with leeks, wine, and loaf. One of the pitchers in which it was served was broken – the handle was broken, as was the lip to same."
2. "The whole robe of the Master was not white, but pearl gray – all combined into one – the gift of Nicodemus to the Lord."
3. "The better looking of the twelve, of course, was Judas, while the younger was John – oval face, dark hair, smooth face – only one with the short hair. Peter, the rough and ready – always that of very short beard, rough and not altogether clean; while Andrew's is just the opposite – very sparse, but inclined to be long more on the side and under the chin – long on the upper lip – his robe was always near gray or black, while his clouts or breeches where striped; while those of Philip and Bartholomew were red and brown"

4. "The Master's hair is most red, inclined to be curly in portions, yet not feminine or weak –STRONG, with heavy piercing eyes that are blue or steel-gray."

5. "His weight would be at least a hundred and seventy pounds. Long tapering fingers, nails well kept. Long nail, though, on the left finger."

6. "Merry – even in the hour of trial. Joke – even in the moment of betrayal."

7. "The sack is empty. Judas departs."

8. "The last is given of the wine and loaf, with which He gives the emblems that should be so dear to every follower of Him. Lays aside His robe, which is all of one piece – girds the towel about His waist, which is dressed with linen that is blue and white. Rolls back the folds, kneel first before John, James, then to Peter – who refuses."

9. "Then the dissertation as to 'He that would be the greatest would be servant to all'."

10. "The basin is taken as without handle, and is made of wood. The water is from the gherkins (gourds), that are in the wide-mouth Shibboleths (streams?) Judges 12:6 that stand in the house of John's father, Zebedee."

11. "And now comes, 'It is finished'."

12. "They sing the ninety-first Psalm, 'He that dwelleth in the secret place of the most high shall abide under the shadow of the Almighty. I will say of the Lord, He is my refuge and my fortress; my God; in Him will I trust."

13. "He is the musician as well, for he uses the harp."

14. "They leave for the garden."

Selected Bibliography

Cayce, Edgar America's most prominent and unusual psychic who had the ability to read the Akashic-Record (Book of life) which contains an imperishable record relating to the earth, the universe, and man since the beginning of time. He gave numerous readings to individuals while in a sleeping-trance covering every conceivable subject. He founded the Association for Research and Enlightenment (A.R.E.) in 1931 which continues to this day to promote the study, application and dissemination of the Information contained in his psychic readings. He was born in 1877 and died in 1945 and during this time period he gave more than 14,000 readings.

Cayce, Hugh Lynn Editor of a four-volume book based upon his father's Readings on the following subjects:

Prophesy

Religion and Psychic Experience

Mysteries of the Mind

Reincarnation

Cranston, Sylvia
Williams, Carey

Author's of Reincarnation – A new horizon in Science, Religion, and Society. Published by Julian Press, New York In 1984.

Furst, Jeffrey

Edgar Cayce's Story of Jesus. Published by The Berkley Publishing Group of New York in 1976.

Laszlo, Ervin

Author of Science and the Akashic Field. Published by Inner Traditions, Rochester, Vermont in 2004.

Montgomery, Ruth

Author of The World Before. Published by Fawcett Crest Books a unit of CBS Publications in 1976.

Todeschi, Kevin

Author of Edgar Cayce on the Akashic Records, published by A.R.E Press, Virginia Beach, Virginia in 1998.

Printed in the United States
By Bookmasters